Goals in Action

21 Days of Goal Setting Through
Daily Devotions

Bailey Guy

Acknowledgements

This book wouldn't be possible without the support, guidance, and inspiration from the people around me. Thank you to the following:

My parents, David and Kelly Guy- You really are the most supportive parents in the world. To my mom, you've always been my biggest cheerleader, and I can't thank you enough for the time and energy you pour into helping me achieve my dreams. To my dad, thank you for wanting to listen to every essay I've ever written and for enthusiastically saying, "You should write a book!," after each one. I love you both!

Jackie Watson- This book would not even exist without the encouragement you've given me. Thank you for answering all my questions, bringing my book cover idea to life, writing a beautiful foreword, and being a fabulous mentor. A million times, thank you!

Amanda Moreno- It's quite fitting that the launch date for this book is February 1, 2022 because it was exactly one year ago on February 1, 2021 that I had the idea for writing it while on the phone with you. Thank you for being a light in my life and reminding me that I CAN do everything I set my mind to.

Thank you to Jasmin Elaine Rojas for capturing the front cover photo and to Carlos Velez for the back cover picture, along with Blake Walters for hair and makeup. You are all so talented!

Grace Glover, Sara Brickell, Elizabeth Graham Pistole, and Shelby Thompson- All of you have impacted my life and been a source of inspiration for a story told in this book. Keep being the world changers that you are!

To you, the reader- Thank you for choosing this book. My hope is that it becomes a place of motivation where you dive deeper into God's purpose for your life. If it is, please reach out! I'd love to hear from you!

Lastly, to Jesus Christ, my Lord and Savior- Thank you for putting this dream in my heart and giving me the courage and motivation to make it happen. This isn't my book, it's our book.

Contents

Foreword

By Jackie B. Watson
Founder & CEO of USA National Miss

It's not every day that one of the girls under my mentorship feels called to write a devotional and I get the distinct honor of helping her achieve this God-given goal. Bailey Guy has a way of bringing the word of God to a very real level that you can relate to as you live your life in pursuit of achieving your own God-given goals.

As I read this devotional, I found myself being renewed by God's word and inspired to always seek God first as I set goals and journey through life. Through the introspective questions in this devotional, I found myself soul searching and being challenged to allow God to chip away at the things I buried deep inside.

God's will is for us to be in His word and to live our daily lives through it. That's exactly what this devotional is about. Bailey shares personal stories you can connect to, while doling out Godly wisdom and insight beyond her years. Real life stories of God's goodness, His faithfulness and His glory fill the pages of this devotional, along with scripture and lots of thought-provoking prompts that guide you along the way as you learn to set goals and live the life you were destined by God to live.

I have no doubt everyone reading this devotional will be inspired and impacted. Bailey's natural story telling ability, coupled with a rich knowledge of God's word, makes this one of the best devotionals for young women I've ever read.

Bailey's devotion to our Lord is a beacon of hope for the next generation who will undoubtedly be impacted by Bailey's insatiable desire to point everyone to our Savior. I'm honored to call her my queen, and sister in Christ.

DEFINE *Success* REDEFINE FAILURE

Week 1: Goal Setting

Day 1: Commit to the Lord

"Commit to the Lord whatever you do, and He will establish your plans."

~ Proverbs 16:3

I've always considered myself a big dreamer. I've always been the girl who had a list of goals I was working towards, and I've found that the most successful goals were the ones I included God in. I've also been competing in pageants for most of my life, and my pageant journey has been something that has greatly strengthened my relationship with God. He's proven His strength through my weaknesses, and I've felt His presence with me on stage. For that reason, I've been intentional about letting God guide my journey through pageants.

When I was 16 years old, I chased one of my biggest dreams: becoming Miss Tennessee Teen USA. Leading up to the pageant, I wanted to include God in every aspect of my preparation. I prayed about every decision and asked that God would lead me. A few days before the pageant began, I made the decision that if I were to win, I wanted to use my reign to grow closer to God and glorify Him with any success I may have. I made a commitment to ensure that I'd be able to do that with the title. I committed to God that if I were to become Miss Tennessee Teen USA, I would read my Bible for at least 10 minutes every single day until Miss Teen USA, no matter how busy or tired I felt.

On October 13, 2018, God decided to put my commitment to the test as I was crowned Miss Tennessee Teen USA 2019. Over the next six months until Miss Teen USA in April 2019, I stayed in the Word daily. It wasn't uncommon for those promised 10 minutes to turn into 30 minutes or an hour. I had never been so intentional about reading my Bible before, and I could feel my faith in God growing every day.

Six months later, I was sitting in my hotel room in Reno-Tahoe, Nevada preparing to check in to Miss Teen USA the next day. I was reading my Bible, just as I'd promised, and God laid something on my heart. He told me that over the next week a lot of people would be watching me, mostly through my Instagram page. And I told God that when people see me, I wanted them to instead see His light shining through me. Right then, I pulled up Instagram on my phone, and I added, "Giving all the glory to God" to my Instagram bio. I made it the first line. It was my hope throughout that week that whoever may visit my Instagram would see God before they saw me.

When you're setting your goals, remember to commit your plans to the Lord, fully trusting that His plan for your life will ultimately prevail.

What is a goal you're currently working towards, and how can you commit your plans to the Lord, allowing Him to establish your steps?

_____

_____

_____

_____

_____

_____

_____

_____

_____

_____

Day 2: Pray for your Enemies

"You have heard that it was said, love your neighbor and hate your enemies. But I tell you, love your enemies and pray for those who persecute you, so that you may be children of your Father in heaven."

~ Matthew 5:44

I'm a strong advocate for women supporting and uplifting each other, and I love being able to pray for my friends and ask God to guide them in their journey to reaching their goals.

But what about praying for the people who may stand in the way of you reaching your own goals?

I want to be crystal clear- I don't see any person as my "enemy," but we all have people in our lives who don't support or believe in us. Whether that person is a friend, family member, teacher, or someone going after the same goal as you, it can hurt when people around us don't want us to succeed.

I recently had a professor who teaches the subject I'm majoring in tell me that I'll never accomplish one of my biggest goals, and that I just don't have what it takes to get there. I was initially in shock as that comment seemed to come out of nowhere. Then I felt hurt that a teacher I've spent so much time learning from doesn't think I'll ever be good enough to see that dream come true. But then I remembered that my professor isn't the one writing my life's story. I'm trusting God to do that.

Instead of getting upset, I prayed for patience and understanding. I wanted to know why my professor felt that way, so I asked. Of course, he couldn't give me any valid reason beyond him just not seeing it happening.

Unfortunately, this isn't a rare occasion. It's very common for people who have big goals to experience someone doubting their abilities and telling them they can't do something.

Next time this happens to you, pray first. Don't react in anger. You'll often find that what they said has nothing to do with your own abilities and everything to do with their personal insecurities. When you see it from that perspective, it's easier to pray for them. Pray that God will not only give you the strength to prove them wrong, but also that He'll heal whatever part of them caused them to say something hurtful to you. We are all God's children, so pray for those who don't support you just as much as you pray for those who do.

Also remember that God has the ultimate say over which of your goals will be reached. Regardless of what anyone says, HIS plan will prevail.

Next time someone doesn't believe in you, how will you react? How can you be praying for those people?

_____

_____

_____

_____

_____

_____

_____

_____

_____

_____

Day 3: Be Courageous

"Have I not commanded you? Be strong and courageous. Do not be frightened, and do not be dismayed for the Lord your God is with you wherever you go."

~ Joshua 1:9

Dreams can be scary. One of my favorite quotes is "If your dreams don't scare you, they're not big enough."

I don't know about you, but sometimes the thought of accomplishing my biggest goals, the things I want to do most in the world, leaves me absolutely terrified. Even the thought of publishing this book scares me.

But God is bigger than my fear. God put this dream in my heart for a reason, and I'm going to pursue it with strength and courage, knowing that God is with me every step of the way. Whatever dream God is setting in your heart right now, don't ignore it, and don't be afraid. The devil uses fear as a weapon to stop you from trusting God's plan. Know that whatever fire God has placed in your heart isn't there by accident. God wants you to take action towards accomplishing your goals.

If you're reading this book right now, that means I completely stepped out of my comfort zone and overcame my fears to publish it. But it's only through God that I have the courage to do this. I pray that you'll have the same courage to fearlessly pursue your own goals.

An excerpt from my personal journal:

I want to use this opportunity to grow closer to my Heavenly Father and tell everyone I can about Him. So although I feel weak and unheard and alone and even though I've lost a lot of my confidence lately, I serve a God that's always greater than anything I face. HE is my strength, HE hears me, HE will never leave my side, and my confidence is found in HIM.

2 Corinthians 5:7 says, "For we walk by faith, not by sight." When I wrote this in my journal, I couldn't see

my goal happening. But I knew God was with me, so I chose to walk not by sight, but by faith.

What is a goal you have that seems scary? Will you choose to pursue it with strength and courage instead of fear?

_____

_____

_____

_____

_____

_____

_____

_____

_____

_____

_____

Day 4: Be Faithful

"Be faithful to the point of death, and I will give you the crown of life."

~ Revelation 2:10

Have you ever been in prayer about something, and then God used a Bible verse to answer your prayer so perfectly in a way that only He can?

It was prelims night at the Miss Tennessee Teen USA 2019 pageant. I had just gotten off the phone with my mom, and I had reviewed the videos my friends had sent of my performances that night. Thoughts of what I could do better for finals the next night were flooding through my mind. I started to pray and thank God for the opportunity to be there, and I told Him I'd be faithful to him throughout the entire process. And then He reminded me that it was getting late, and I still hadn't read my Bible.

I looked over at my roommate, a girl I had become good friends with through pageants, and I wondered what she'd think if she saw me get my Bible out. We had prayed together before prelims, but I for some reason worried that she'd think I was weird for bringing out all my pens and highlighters to read my Bible. I thought, 'Maybe I just won't tonight.'

But then I felt God say, "Don't deny me."

Even though I was scared to, I got my Bible out, and God led me to a page in Revelation. My eyes landed on a verse, Revelation 2:10, the one I used for today. I had just told God I'd be faithful, and here was a verse telling me God would give me the crown of life for it.

Then I got to Revelation 3:8, "I have placed before you an open door that no one can close because you have but little power; yet you have kept my word and have not denied my name." I felt like God was speaking directly to me, and I could feel Him smiling down on me because I hadn't denied Him. I had been faithful.

It was in that moment that I realized the next night's outcome didn't matter. It was never really about that metal and rhinestone crown. If I'm not pursuing the crown of life I'll receive in heaven someday, every other crown or goal I pursue on earth is meaningless.

Whatever your goals are, and in any success you achieve, remember to always keep God first. Never deny His name; He's the one who got you there.

As you pursue your goals, what are some ways you can show the world that your faith is in God?

_____

_____

_____

_____

_____

_____

_____

_____

_____

_____

_____

Day 5: The Potter and the Clay

"I went down to the potter's house, and there he was, working away at the wheel. But the jar that he was making from the clay became flawed in the potter's hand, so he made it into another jar, as it seemed right for him to do. The word of the Lord came to me: 'House of Israel, can I not treat you as this potter treats the clay?' This is the Lord's declaration, 'Just like clay in the potter's hand, so are you in my hand.'"

~ Jeremiah 18:3-6

Have you ever had a goal you wanted so badly to achieve, but you just didn't feel ready, capable, or good enough to do it?

On July 10, 2021, one of my biggest dreams came true as I was crowned USA National Teen. Everyone there saw my crowning moment, but no one saw the self-doubt that was in my heart. I'm going to tell you what you didn't see on stage or on social media, because my journey to the national crown was anything but confident.

In the months leading up to nationals, I had never felt more anxiety. Something in my mind was constantly telling me, "You can't do this," and I was starting to believe it. I couldn't practice my gown or runway walk for more than a few minutes at a time before feeling like a weight was pushing on my chest, making it hard to even breathe. Every time I practiced for my interview, I would break down in tears wondering if I wasn't where God wanted me to be.

My mom reminded me that thieves don't break into empty houses, and that this anxiety was NOT from God but instead was a spiritual attack from the devil because he knew what I was capable of achieving. He tried everything he could to stop me, and it almost worked. Just two months before nationals, I told my mom I thought I should drop out.

Thankfully she convinced me not to, but that self-doubt didn't go away. I decided I needed to fully trust God and give all my worries to Him.

Leading up to the pageant, I wrote this prayer in my journal:

> *Lord, please guide me in my preparations and lead me every step of the way. Please let your voice be always present in my life and give me the motivation to work towards my goals every single day. Please mold my heart to be exactly what you want it to be and give me opportunities to encourage and uplift the people around me. Lord, I trust in you. Please do your work in and through my life. Amen.*

I couldn't do it alone. I didn't feel ready, capable, or good enough. And without God, I wasn't. I needed God to mold me like a potter does with clay. God gave me the strength to overcome everything standing in my way.

What are some areas of your life you need to give to God so He can mold you into his perfect vision?

_____

_____

_____

_____

_____

_____

_____

_____

_____

_____

_____

Day 6: Trust in God

"Blessed is the one who trusts in the Lord, whose confidence is in Him."

~ Jeremiah 17:7

Have you ever wanted to tell God what you think His plan should be, even though you know His plan is always greater than yours? Whenever I find myself doing that, God reminds me to simply trust in Him.

I remember being at USA National Miss nationals, and I kept wanting God to just tell me why I was there. Because of all the anxiety and self-doubt I had faced for the months leading up to nationals, I was 99.9% sure His plan did not include me winning. But God doesn't need us to know or understand His plan, He just wants us to trust it.

I wrote this in my journal on July 9, 2021, the night before I was crowned USA National Teen:

I think through this process, God is teaching me how to trust Him. And not just "trust that I'll win," but trust that God's got me even if I don't. God sees what I can't see. He knows my future, and He knows what I need to get there. I'm trusting that God's plan is perfect and always better than mine.

Of course I wanted to win, but I had to trust that God's plan was better than whatever I wanted. When you're working towards a goal, God may allow things to happen that you don't understand.

Jesus said in John 13:7, "You don't understand now what I'm doing, but someday you will."

I didn't understand at the time why God was letting me go through that, but I chose to trust in His plan regardless. I now see that while the devil was trying to knock me down and make me lose all my confidence, it was really just shifting my focus. God allowed me to lose my confidence so I could find it in Him.

As you set and chase your goals, you're bound to face obstacles. In the moment, it's easy to wonder why

God would allow that to be part of the plan. Next time that happens, remind yourself that God sees what you can't see. What may be a setback now could lead to a comeback later. God is always working. Trust in Him.

What are some obstacles you're currently facing on the journey to your goals? Will you trust in God to get you through it?

_____

_____

_____

_____

_____

_____

_____

_____

_____

_____

_____

Day 7: Plan for your Goals

"Suppose one of you wants to build a tower. Won't you first sit down and estimate the cost to see if you have enough money to complete it?"

~ Luke 14:28

"Do you not know that in a race all the runners run, but only one gets the prize? Run in such a way as to get the prize."

~ 1 Corinthians 9:24

Goal setting is one of my biggest keys to success. I believe planning and preparing for your goals, just as the above verses suggest, is a crucial step in achieving them.

One of my biggest goals going into college was to be selected as a President's Ambassador, the most prestigious program for students at my school. The President's Ambassadors have the opportunity to attend exclusive board meetings and dinners, speak at special events, serve as the official tour guides, and receive a full tuition scholarship.

But before I could become a President's Ambassador, I had to plan and set goals for that bigger goal to happen. My first step was to write my goal down and pray about it. Then I learned everything I could about the program. This helped me discover my "why" and determine what I had to offer. I also put extra effort into making sure my grades and school involvement aligned with what the President's Ambassadors represented.

After three rounds of interviews in the selection process, I finally achieved my goal of becoming a President's Ambassador. But without all the planning and preparation, I wouldn't have been ready for those interviews.

Whatever your goal is, start planning for it now. Think through everything you need for your goal to happen. How will you obtain those things along the way? Remember to not just plan for how you'll achieve your goal, also think through what you'll do after you get it. How will achieving your goal allow you to help other people?

Plan, prepare, work hard, and remember that with God, all things are possible.

What can you be doing now to prepare for your goal, and what is your plan for after your goal is achieved?

_____

_____

_____

_____

_____

_____

_____

_____

_____

_____

_____

DEFINE

Success

REDEFINE

FAILURE

Week 2: Failure

Day 8: The Lord Sees the Heart

"Humans do not see what the Lord sees, for humans see what is visible, but the Lord sees the heart."

~ 1 Samuel 16:7

Some goals, no matter how much we plan and prepare for them, just aren't in God's will to happen. But that doesn't mean we failed for trying.

During my junior year of high school, I took the ACT test, which is the standardized test used for college admissions. Students are given a score on a scale from 1-36, and that score can be a determining factor for where a student goes to college and what scholarships are available to them.

Going into the test, I had a goal in mind of what I wanted my score to be. I had studied and taken ACT prep classes, and I felt ready to achieve that score. But when I got my test results back, I had scored three points lower than my goal. I felt like I'd failed because I hadn't reached the score I had in mind, but that night God revealed something to me through 1 Samuel 16:7, today's verse.

I realized that even though I felt like I'd failed, God didn't see me as a failure at all. Those test questions were written by people and scored based on my abilities in math, science, English, and reading. God doesn't score us on a scale from 1-36. He doesn't judge us based on our academic performances, or any of our earthly accomplishments for that matter. He knows His children are worth so much more than that.

God reminded me that night of how worthy I am in His eyes. He loves me so much that He sent his one and only Son to die on a cross for me. Jesus didn't do that based on my grades or test scores. Jesus gave His life because He loves me. No success or failure I have will ever change that.

Next time you have a goal that just doesn't get accomplished, remember that God doesn't see you as a failure. He made you for a reason and gave you worth and purpose that can't be taken away. God sees your heart and how much love you give to the people around you, and for that your life is already a beautiful success story.

Are there any unrealized goals you've had that are weighing you down? How can you give those to God instead and see yourself how God sees you?

_____

_____

_____

_____

_____

_____

_____

_____

_____

_____

_____

_____

Day 9: Your Support System

"Plans fail for lack of counsel, but with many advisors they succeed."

~ Proverbs 15:22

I often get asked if I have any "pageant horror stories." Well, this is definitely one of them.

At 14 years old, I was one of the youngest contestants competing in one of Tennessee's biggest teen state pageants. We were in the middle of the final show, and I was backstage in my blue silk evening gown just moments away from being lined up to compete. As I looked in the dressing room mirror, I noticed that my spray tan was looking a bit splotchy on my right shoulder. The girl next to me was holding a bottle of Sally Hansen "Airbrush Legs" body makeup, and she kindly let me borrow it. I'd never used it before, but I was in complete shock when instead of slowly coming out onto my hand, the nozzle spewed tan makeup all over the front of my gown.

I ran to the backstage chaperones, pleading for help, but all they could say was, "Sorry, you'll have to get that professionally cleaned out when you get back home." I frantically went back to the mirror, starting to cry and feeling completely hopeless.

But then I heard someone call my name. I turned around and saw my friend Elizabeth coming towards me with a Mr. Clean magic eraser sponge. I took a step back and said, "No, no, no," because I was scared it might do even more damage.

But she calmly said, "Trust me." She rubbed the sponge against the makeup stain, and within seconds it was completely unnoticeable. I gave her a giant hug and thanked her as we both ran to get in line to compete in evening gown.

The people you surround yourself with really do affect your ability to achieve your goals. What could've easily turned into a failure (and extremely embarrassing moment for me) didn't because I had the right person around me who helped me succeed. When it's time to go for your goals, make sure the people around you are ones who love and support you and will pick you back up if you fall. Pray that God puts the right people in your life to be there for you.

And as for Elizabeth, she's now Miss Tennessee USA and just recently made Top 16 at Miss USA! She was there for me when she didn't have to be, and one of my goals is to show the same kindness to the people around me that she showed to me that day.

Who is your support system of family, friends, and advisors who are there for you as you pursue your dreams?

_____

_____

_____

_____

_____

_____

_____

_____

_____

_____

_____

Day 10: Repositioning

"For we are God's handiwork, created in Christ Jesus to do good works, which God prepared in advance for us to do."

~ Ephesians 2:10

All throughout middle school and high school, I had one main goal: to be on student council.

Starting in 7th grade, I ran for student council every single year. My mom and I would go to Dollar General before the election and pick out colorful posterboards and stickers and decorations for them, and I'd even attach lights to all my posters. We'd have an annual 2-person student council poster party in my living room as we carefully crafted the allotted five posters every year. We used puns like, "Vote Bailey Guy! It just makes *cents*!" on my poster surrounded by fake dollars and coins when I ran for treasurer, and one year I even handmade a rubber band bracelet for each student in my grade on my Rainbow Loom to go with my campaign slogan, "*Band* together and vote Bailey Guy!" I really wanted to be on student council.

Every single year I put my whole heart into my student council campaign, handing out bookmarks and asking each person for their vote. And every single year, I lost. I always came so close, and some years the difference was by less than five votes. Every year I begged God to let me win, just once, but it was never His plan.

Then when I was in 10th grade, I came to a realization. Despite never winning a single election, everyone *thought* I was on student council. They'd ask me about the Homecoming dress up days and what games would be played at the pep rallies, and I'd always either know the answer or ask someone who did and get back to them. Then they'd thank me and comment on how happy they were to have a friend on student council.

What God showed me through those years of failing to be on student council was that I don't need a title to be a servant. I didn't need to be the student council president to help make my school a better place. I could make a difference as just Bailey. The same is true for you. You don't have to have a title or fancy position to make an impact.

Just like God, my school didn't see me as a failure either. In 12th grade, the same people who had watched me fail since 7th grade voted me for the senior superlative, "Most Likely to Succeed." I've found that sometimes what may seem like a failure is really just a reposition.

What are some ways you can positively impact people right where you are?

_____

_____

_____

_____

_____

_____

_____

_____

_____

_____

_____

Day 11: He Qualifies the Called

"If you have faith the size of a mustard seed, you can say to this mountain, 'Move from here to there,' and it will move. Nothing will be impossible for you."

~ Matthew 17:20

If someone would've told me five years ago that today I'd be writing a devotional, I would've never believed them. That's because while myself and my family are all Christians, I actually didn't grow up consistently going to church. We usually went to church on holidays, I loved going to Vacation Bible School every year, and I'd occasionally go with my aunt, but other than that, going to church wasn't a big part of my childhood.

For that reason, I often felt unqualified to talk about God with people outside of my family. I was afraid I didn't know enough to be able to make a difference, and that caused me to stay silent in opportunities when I could've shared what I did know.

It wasn't until one of my best friends, Grace, reminded me of a quote that changed my entire perspective. She told me, "God doesn't call on the qualified; He qualifies the called."

I didn't always feel qualified, but I did feel called. I realized that God's calling alone is what qualifies me to step out of my comfort zone and do things I never thought I could. Things like sharing my testimony or telling people what God was doing in my life seemed like a mountain I'd never be able to move. But where I lacked in confidence, I was strong in faith.

Often our goals and the things God is calling us to do can feel like a mountain, but remember that with faith the size of a mustard seed, you can move those mountains. With God, nothing will be impossible for you.

Don't let the feeling of being unqualified stop you from chasing your goals. Know that whatever God is calling you to do, He's calling YOU to do it. He knows you better than anyone, and He still chose you, exactly as you are, for His plan.

Have you ever felt unqualified to fulfill what God is calling you to do? What are some mountains you're trying to move?

_____

_____

_____

_____

_____

_____

_____

_____

_____

_____

_____

Day 12: His Plan is Greater

"'For I know the plans I have for you,' declares the Lord, 'plans to prosper you and not to harm you, plans to give you hope and a future.'"

~ Jeremiah 29:11

I remember having a lot of goals and events I was looking forward to for my senior year of high school. There were club competitions I was preparing for, my senior tennis season, prom, and of course graduation.

But then March 13, 2020, happened... the day President Trump declared America was in a national state of emergency due to COVID-19. Unknowingly at the time, it also ended up being my last day of high school.

As a Class of 2020 senior, I could only describe the months that followed that day as complete heartbreak. All the plans I had for how I'd finish high school were cancelled as every person in the world was personally affected by the pandemic. Even though it was completely out of my control, I still felt the feeling of failure for not getting to accomplish the goals I'd set for the spring and summer of 2020. But in the midst of that heartbreak, God reminded me that He was still right there with me. He had plans for me bigger than I could imagine.

Sometimes we have plans that just don't work out. Whether it was to win a certain competition, or make a team, or get chosen for a job we feel perfect for, sometimes God has a different plan.

There's an old quote that says, "Write your plans in pencil, and give God the eraser." No matter how much we plan and prepare for a goal to happen, God is the ultimate decision maker.

When you face failure or have to watch your plans fall apart, lean into God and know that what He has in store is always greater. His plans are to prosper you and give you hope and a future.

Write about a time when God's plan proved to be greater than your own.

_____

_____

_____

_____

_____

_____

_____

_____

_____

_____

_____

_____

Day 13: Wonderfully Made

"I praise you because I am fearfully and wonderfully made; your works are wonderful; I know that full well."

~ Psalm 139:14

Sometimes we fail ourselves with negative self-talk. Last year while I was competing at a state pageant, I learned what a difference it can make when we change the way we talk to and about ourselves. This pageant had an opening number dance, and let's just say God decided my talents would be better suited OFF the dance floor.

The girl next to me in the dance rehearsal was named Sara, and we quickly became best friends throughout that weekend. She's truly one of the most talented people I've ever met, and I'm convinced there's nothing she can't do- including dancing.

I, on the other hand, felt like a baby deer that didn't know how to walk yet. After trying (and failing) to get the dance down, I started to tell Sara that I'm a terrible dancer.

Sara stopped me and said, "Don't say that. Only positivity here. Now you have to list three things you like about yourself!"

I can't even put into words how much better that made me feel, and I've carried her advice with me ever since. Every time I catch myself starting to talk negatively about myself or thinking I'll fail, I replace those thoughts with three positive things about myself.

When you're going for a goal, it can be easy to compare yourself to the people next to you and believe you just don't measure up. But don't let yourself be your own biggest enemy- that mindset isn't setting you up for success.

God has given each of us our own talents and gifts, and He didn't make a mistake when making you. God has given you everything you need to succeed in fulfilling His purpose for your life. Talking bad about yourself is talking bad about one of God's creations that He loves so much. It's not pleasing to God, and it's not good for your spirit either. You are fearfully and

wonderfully made, and every detail is exactly how God
intended.

What are three things you like about yourself? In what ways can you use those things to serve God?

_____

_____

_____

_____

_____

_____

_____

_____

_____

_____

_____

_____

Day 14: Failure is Never Final

"Though he may stumble, he will not fall, for the Lord upholds him with His hand."

~ Psalm 37:24

"He has made everything beautiful in its time."

~ Ecclesiastes 3:11

We've all faced failure. We've all heard "no" when we wanted a "yes," or worked hard for a crown that went to someone else or had a goal that just didn't work out when we wanted it to. I'm a firm believer that failure isn't the opposite of success. Instead, it's part of success. What we may see as a failure in the moment may really just be part of the success story God has written for us.

Awhile back, I was a state titleholder for a pageant system that had a personal introduction competition. Two weeks after winning the Tennessee title, I traveled to Alabama as "visiting royalty" at their state pageant, and all current titleholders were asked to deliver their personal introductions on stage.

I felt confident as I walked up to the mic, but after the first line of my introduction, my mind went completely blank. I tried starting over from the beginning, but once again, my words got jumbled and I couldn't remember anything I'd practiced and prepared to say. To make things worse, the one thing I did get out was about how much I like public speaking. Talk about embarrassing! When I decided I was past the point of recovering from this mishap, I wrapped it up and practically ran off the stage. It felt like a major fail.

Three months later at the national pageant, I competed in personal introduction once again. I'd practiced a million times, specifically because I didn't want to repeat what happened in Alabama. I was standing backstage practicing my introduction in my head, minutes from saying it in front of the judges and audience. There were only three girls in front of me before it'd be my turn to go onstage when all of a sudden, my mind blanked again. I couldn't remember anything past the first line! My heart was racing as I got out of line, ran past the choreographer and out of the ballroom, and down the hallway into the ballroom I'd been in earlier that day. I found the copy of my printed-out introduction that I'd left in there, and I ran all the way back down the hallway and into line, praying I hadn't missed my turn. There was one girl in front of me when I got back in line, so I got to read over my introduction one time before going onstage.

I didn't win that pageant, but when I got my scores back I was shocked to see that I'd had the highest score in introduction out of my entire division! I really believe God allowed me to "fail" in Alabama so I'd work even harder leading up to nationals. That failure led to a bigger success. God knows exactly what you need. Trust that His plan is greater, even if it includes a few "failures" along the way.

Write about a time when a "failure" taught you a bigger lesson than success would have.

_____

_____

_____

_____

_____

_____

_____

_____

_____

_____

_____

_____

DEFINE
Success
REDEFINE
FAILURE

Week 3: Success

Day 15: Overflow with God's Joy

"May the God of hope fill you with all joy and peace as you trust in him, so that you may overflow with hope by the power of the Holy Spirit."

~ Romans 15:13

I should've been at the most confident point of my life. I had just won Miss Tennessee Teen USA 2019, a goal I'd worked hard for so many years to achieve. So why did I feel so empty?

I thought reaching "success" and accomplishing my biggest goal at the time would make everything in my life perfect. I had the mindset of, "If I could just have (insert title, job, financial milestone, relationship, social status, etc.), then all my problems will go away."

But I'll let you in on a little secret: success doesn't make you whole. I thought winning a big title would make all my insecurities vanish, but in reality, it only magnified them. The months following my win weren't the perfect and happy life that's talked about or portrayed on social media. They were filled with comparison to other current and past titleholders and thinking I wasn't pretty enough, smart enough, or good enough to hold the title God had just blessed me with. I looked at my first runner up and wondered if the judges had made the wrong choice.

But God makes no mistakes. And I knew the only thing that could fill me was the joy that can only come from God. On the very first day of this devotional, I told you about the commitment I'd made to read my Bible every single day as Miss Tennessee Teen USA. I truly believe the fulfillment of that promise was the key to reframing my perspective. I was in a place of allowing other people's opinions to determine my value, but being in the Word and reading about Jesus's love every single day filled me with joy. It reminded me of who I am, and more importantly, Whose I am.

If there's a goal you've been working towards for years now, hoping that it will fill a void inside you once you reach it, I want you to know that only God can do that. No crown or title or success can fill you. You have to already be full and know that you're just as worthy before you have the crown as you will be after. Know that you're a child of the highest King, and that's a title no one can take away from you. After all, they aren't the ones who gave it to you.

What's a Bible verse or reminder from God that always fills you with joy whenever you see it?

_____

_____

_____

_____

_____

_____

_____

_____

_____

_____

_____

Day 16: Go Where God Sends You

"But I protested, 'Oh no, Lord God! Look, I don't know how to speak since I am only a youth.' Then the Lord said to me: Do not say, 'I am only a youth' for you will go to everyone I send you to and speak whatever I tell you."

~ Jeremiah 1:6-7

What does success mean to you? For me, anyone who is living their God-given purpose and following the Lord's commands is successful.

Back in high school, God taught me a really important lesson when I least expected it. I was running up the stairs of my high school one morning, minutes away from being late to my first class. But in the crowd of students, I noticed a boy I'd never seen before. He was sitting on the stairs alone.

I hoped he was okay as I kept rushing to class. But then as I was heading down the hallway past the stairs, God gave me a command that literally stopped me in my tracks. He told me to go back to that boy.

"But God, I'm about to be late to class," I argued.

Still, God was telling me to go back. I turned around and headed back to the stairs as the late bell for my first class rang. The boy was still sitting on the stairs, which were now empty. I sat down next to him and asked if he was okay, but he wouldn't tell me anything. So we just sat in silence for a minute until I said, "I just wanted to make sure you're alright. And I hope you have a good day."

As I walked to class, I asked God, "What was that about? He didn't even say anything." I couldn't understand why God had asked me to do that when from my perspective, nothing happened. But then God brought a story to my mind that a teacher had told me years prior about a boy who was suffering from suicidal thoughts and planning to end his life after school when a group of other boys unexpectedly invited him to play football with them later that day, and that small gesture saved the boy's life and convinced him to keep going. Tears started streaming down my face as I felt the gravity of the moment. I'll probably never know what that boy on the stairs was experiencing in that moment, but I know God made a difference through me.

I felt a different kind of success. There wasn't an award or any recognition given, and no one else even knew what had happened, but I could feel God smiling down at me for the rest of the day. I had successfully completed a mission I didn't know I'd be called to.

As you make your way through this crazy journey of life, never lose sight of our ultimate goal as Christians: to strive to be more like Jesus and less like ourselves. You may never have the crown, job, relationship, or anything else you want, but you will always be successful if God is the one leading your life.

What is your definition of success?

_____

_____

_____

_____

_____

_____

_____

_____

_____

_____

_____

_____

Day 17: Impact

"Perhaps you have come to your royal position for such a time as this."

~ Esther 4:14

Queen Esther is one of my favorite women in the Bible. After all, she even became queen through the first recorded beauty pageant! She then used her royal position to soften the king's heart and save the Jewish people from genocide.

As children of the King, we are all called to a royal position as well. We can have an extraordinary impact on the world just like Esther did.

When I was 6 years old, I was diagnosed with scoliosis, which is an abnormal curvature of the spine. My curve was at a 40-degree angle upon diagnosis, but by the time I had the spinal fusion surgery at age 11, it had already escalated to a 90 degree curve. It was one of the hardest times of my life, but through it I learned the impact one person can make.

On my third day in the hospital, Miss Tennessee 2013 Shelby Thompson came to visit me. She didn't just pop in for a picture, she stayed by my bed and talked to me for 3.5 hours! She told me what it's like competing at Miss America, and I told her what it's like being in 6th grade. Over those 3.5 hours, I forgot that I was in the hospital. I forgot that I'd have to miss the next two months of school for recovery. I forgot about the back brace, the appointments, and the pain. That visit may have been a small part of her day as Miss Tennessee, but it meant the world to me as a little girl in the hospital.

I decided that day that with every success I have in life, I want to use it to make an impact on others how Shelby did for me. I saw firsthand what a difference a girl with a crown can make, and I've never let go of that vision.

With every success God blesses you with, you are given an opportunity to make an impact. Whatever your position is, whether as an athlete, business owner, or even as a queen, think about why God put you there. He didn't do it on accident.

What positions do you hold right now? How can you use that to make an impact on others?

_____

_____

_____

_____

_____

_____

_____

_____

_____

_____

_____

_____

Day 18: God Works All Things for Good

"And we know that in all things God works for the good of those who love him, who have been called according to his purpose."

~ Romans 8:28

I woke up on finals day of USA National Miss nationals feeling anything but ready to compete that night. I had a runny nose and sore throat, and I could feel it getting worse as the day went on. Just a few hours before finals started, I couldn't talk louder than a whisper. My mom gave me hot tea and vitamin C, and I stuffed tissues and cough drops into the pockets of my evening gown before heading to the final show.

After making Top 6 and re-competing in gown, I was worried about the possibility of making Top 3 and losing my voice again during onstage question. This is what I later wrote in my journal about that moment:

I had a lot of downtime during the intermission, so I found a secluded area backstage and started to pray. I told God that I 100% trusted His plan, and I surrendered the results to Him. Then I opened my eyes, and I could visualize the crown at a distance in front of me. I physically started walking forward, imagining myself stepping closer and closer to the crown. It felt so real. I even held my arms out, as if I was reaching out to this imaginary crown in front of me, and then I prayed again and told God that if it's for me, that I accept it, and I'm ready to be the next USA National Teen.

After intermission, it was time for the Top 3 announcement and onstage question. To my surprise, I was the first name called into Top 3. The biggest critique I had gotten while practicing for both interview and onstage question leading up to nationals was that I talk way too fast. But while answering my onstage question, I was so worried about losing my voice again that I talked way slower than normal. I realized during my answer that slowing down was actually calming my nerves and allowing me to think clearly and confidently about what I wanted to say.

When I first woke up that morning, I couldn't understand why God would allow me to feel sick on such an important day, but while speaking into the microphone that night, it all made sense. My voice came back just in time, and being sick gave me a reason to slow down and just trust Him. God had a purpose for me that night, and He worked ALL things (even a sore throat and runny nose) for my good.

When was a time God worked everything together for your good, even if you didn't understand in the moment what He was doing?

_____

_____

_____

_____

_____

_____

_____

_____

_____

_____

_____

Day 19: Give

"Give, and it will be given to you. A good measure, pressed down, shaken together and running over, will be poured into your lap. For with the measure you use, it will be measured to you."

~ Luke 6:38

"Each of you should use whatever gift you have received to serve others, as faithful stewards of God's grace in its various forms."

~ 1 Peter 4:10

I like to count my blessings pretty regularly. Any time I'm feeling down, pulling out a pen and paper to list out things I'm grateful for always lifts my spirits. This practice also helps me realize how much I have to then give to others. Reframing your mindset to look for ways you can give instead of receive will truly fill your heart with joy from Jesus. After all, Jesus was the greatest giver of all. He gave His LIFE for yours.

I encourage you to look for ways you can use your success to give. One of my favorite memories as Miss Tennessee Teen USA was setting a goal of donating 2,000 books to kids across Tennessee, but after being so blessed by help from my friends and community, I was able to collect and donate over 5,000 books that year!

If you don't have money or resources to give, giving your time is so important as well. Reading to kids in after school programs, volunteering at an animal shelter or nursing home, and participating in charity events are all great ways to give your time.

Something I realized recently is that one of the most powerful things I have to give is my story. Through telling about my experiences, I can relate to someone and encourage them in their own life. This can be done with a social media post, at lunch with a friend who needs uplifting, or even with a stranger that God leads you to talk to at work or school.

Whatever gifts God has given you, use them to give. If you can sing or dance, give your talents to an event in your community. If you're really good at math, offer to tutor someone you know could use your help.

Every time you give, do it as a form of worship to God. Ask Him for opportunities to use your gifts, talents, and success to help others, and He will lead you to the people who need you.

Who do you feel called to serve? How can you use your gifts, talents, and success to give to them?

_____

_____

_____

_____

_____

_____

_____

_____

_____

_____

_____

Day 20: Endurance

"Brothers and sisters, I do not consider myself yet to have taken hold of it. But one thing I do: Forgetting what is behind and straining toward what is ahead, I press on toward the goal to win the prize for which God has called me heavenward in Christ Jesus."

~ Philippians 3:13-14

"Therefore, since we are surrounded by such a great cloud of witnesses, let us throw off everything that hinders and the sin that so easily entangles. And let us run with perseverance the race marked out for us, fixing our eyes on Jesus, the pioneer and perfecter of faith. For the joy that lay before him, he endured the cross, despising the shame, and sat down at the right hand of the throne of God."

~ Hebrews 12:1-2

God has a plan for you. He put you exactly where you are for a reason. I believe the greatest success is fulfilling that plan and living out God's purpose for your life. All throughout your life, you're going to encounter trials and tribulations that will test your trust in God.

One of the biggest challenges I've faced is comparison. It's so easy to compare where you are and what you have to someone else, but think about this: would you compare God's plan for your life to His plan for someone else's life and tell Him you'd rather have the plan He set for that other person?

What He has planned for them is for THEM. And what He has planned for you is for YOU. There's no need to compare. Even if you did, it wouldn't be a fair comparison. One thing every successful person you see has in common is a long list of losses you don't see. Comparing yourself to someone else's success without considering or even knowing their losses doesn't get you any farther in the race God has for you.

People could look at my life and see that I was Miss Tennessee Teen USA at 16, but they don't see that I didn't even make Top 15 on that same stage when I was 14.

People could see that I'm now USA National Teen but not see that it took me four years to win my very first pageant or that it took another three years after that before I ever won a state title.

If you want to be successful, you have to endure the losses. Failure isn't the opposite of success; it's a part of it. Just as Colossians 3:2 says, "Set your minds on things above, not on earthly things." Don't focus on the obstacles and setbacks, keep your eyes on Jesus and trust that He'll carry you through them.

What trials have you faced and overcome in your life?

_____

_____

_____

_____

_____

_____

_____

_____

_____

_____

_____

Day 21: God Will Open the Door

"You shall eat the fruit of the labor of your hands; you shall be blessed, and it shall be well with you."

~ Psalm 128:2

"I know your works. Behold, I have set before you an open door, which no one is able to close. I know that you have but little power, and yet you have kept my word and have not denied my name."

~ Revelation 3:8

When you're following God's calling for your life, you will be successful. You can't fail at something you were born to do, but you have to be working towards it. All my life my mom has reminded me of the message in Galatians 6:7, "You reap what you sow." Whatever you focus your time and energy on will grow.

Leading up to USA National Miss nationals, I didn't believe I had a single chance at winning. But I knew that God had placed me on that path for a reason, so I worked hard to prepare myself to do my best anyway. I realized that I was looking at my goal of winning nationals as something that was unattainable, something so far out of reach. The most important work I had to do wasn't finding the perfect wardrobe or practicing my walk for hours (although those were important steps too). The real work was what was going on in my head. I had to overcome this idea that I wasn't good enough in order to rise up and be the woman God made me to be.

When I came to the conclusion that I was trusting the voice in my head saying, "I can't," more than I was trusting God's reason for putting me there, I knew I had to make a change. I love having visual reminders of my goals, so in the months leading up to nationals, I put sticky notes on my mirror that said, "I am USA National Teen," and I read them out loud every morning. I didn't always believe it, but I said it anyway.

When you fully trust God to guide you, and you take the right steps in His direction, don't be surprised when opportunities and success come to you. If I had accepted and believed the voice in my head telling me I'd never be USA National Teen, I may have taken myself out of the race before it even began. Instead, I worked to be mentally prepared for whatever God had in store. Whatever God's plan for your life is, He handpicked you out of 7.9 billion people to complete that mission. You have to believe that YOU are the best person to fulfill the plans God has for you, and then put in the work to make them happen. Not working hard for the goals God sets in your heart is directly going against His plan. God will open the door, but it's up to you to walk through it. Work hard, trust God, and put those goals into action!

Your life is already a success story for pursuing your God-given purpose. What affirmations can you tell yourself when you need to be reminded of that?

_____

_____

_____

_____

_____

_____

_____

_____

_____

_____

_____

_____

Made in the USA
Las Vegas, NV
04 August 2024

93349000R00056